CLAY BOTS!

This edition published in 2015
By SpiceBox™
12171 Horseshoe Way
Richmond, BC
Canada V7A 4V4

Copyright © SpiceBox™ 2015

ISBN 10: 1-77132-351-5
ISBN 13: 978-1-77132-351-2

CEO and Publisher: Ben Lotfi
Editorial: Ania Jaraczewski
Creative Director: Garett Chan
Art Director: Christine Covert
Design, Illustration & Photography: Charmaine Muzyka
Production: James Badger, Mell D'Clute
Sourcing: Janny Lam, Sherry Xie

For more SpiceBox products and information, visit our website:
www.spiceboxbooks.com

Manufactured in China

1 3 5 7 9 10 8 6 4 2

Contents

Amazing Clay	5
Tools & Materials	6
Tips & Techniques	8
Wind-up Fun	11
Annie Argh	12
Zappi	14
Steve McBolt	16
Sayonara Sam	18
Bob the Blob	20
Lizzie	22
Felix	24
Wanda	26
Monty	28
Marcus	30
Dotty	32
Luella	34
Space Rover	36
Garett	38
Robbie	40
Bort	42
Squiggy	44
Making Plants	46

Amazing Clay

Clay can be magically transformed from a few shapeless lumps into all kinds of amazing things! You can even make your own wind-up toys using the mechanical feet included in the kit. Use your imagination to dream up your own awesome aliens, monsters and robots in crazy colors! Give them three eyes, six arms, spots, stripes and wires — whatever you want. Then have fun watching your creations walk on their own! Check out the projects in this book and try out some of the tricks and techniques we used to make our clay characters, then get creative and have fun making your own fantastic creations. With the easy, air-drying clay in the kit, you can do just about anything!

Tools & Materials

Cool clay

Air-drying clay will harden on its own after you've finished molding it. And it will still look exactly the way you made it!

Wax paper

Not that you would ever make a mess, but it's still a good idea to put wax paper or a plastic mat over your work surface. This will also keep your projects from picking up dirt so your creatures won't all turn into dust bunnies!

Dowel

The clay is pretty sticky and might stick to wood. To roll it out, either use a plastic dowel or cover the clay with parchment paper if using a wooden rolling pin.

Shaping Tools

You can make little holes and lines using different tools. Check out my nifty seams — they were made with the pointy tool!

Go wild!

Because you don't have to bake the clay, you can stick all kinds of things into it: beads, buttons, twigs, fabric, sparkles, bits of wire and pipe cleaners. Once the clay has dried, you can also paint or draw on it. Be creative!

Tips & Techniques

Before you start

Here are a few tips that every clay artist should read before they embark on their clay-making adventures:

Don't eat the clay! Even though this clay is non-toxic, make sure to keep it away from pets and younger siblings.

I see those crumbs on your fingers! Unless you want them to become part of your project, you'd better wash your hands first! I'm watching you!

Keep it sealed

You don't want your clay drying out before your masterpiece is finished, so make sure you keep whatever you're not using in a plastic bag or container. Only take out small bits at a time.

Clay rescue

If the clay does start to feel dry, all is not lost! Work a few drops of water into it until it's easy to mold again.

The need to knead

Knead the clay for a minute or so to make it soft and easy to use.

The projects will give you lots of ideas, but be creative and change up the colors, or make stripes instead of spots...whatever you feel like doing!

actual size pair of eyes:

Bits & pieces

All the creations in this book were made using very small amounts of clay. A little goes a long way!

Mixing colors

Don't have the color you need? Don't worry! You can mix two or more colors together to make any color you want. Just add small bits of color together and work the clay until you get the shade you want. If you want stripes or swirls, mix the clay just a little bit, so you can still see the different colors.

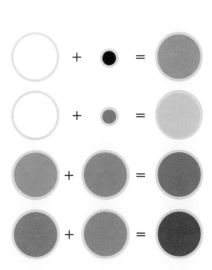

Tips & Techniques

Simple shapes

The characters and objects in the book may look hard to make, but they were all put together from very simple shapes — like a round ball for a body and flat circles for ears. Easy! Each project will show you which shapes you need. It's a good idea to make all the shapes before you start sticking them together. That way it's easier to make sure that each shape is the right size.

Making a teardrop shape

Many of the projects in this book use "teardrop" shapes. To make this shape, first roll the clay into a ball. Then pinch out one end and roll that end back and forth a few times until you have a shape that looks like a drop of water.

Hey, who are you calling round?

Drying time

Once you've finished your project, leave it to dry for at least 24 hours. Then your cool clay creation is done!

Wind-up Fun!

This fun contraption is what you'll use to make creations that walk on their own! All you need to do is mold a layer of clay over the cone shape and then attach all the parts of your monster, robot or alien. Use the rolling pin to make a nice flat piece of clay about 4 x 1.5 inches wide, then wrap it around the form and smooth out the seam with your finger. If you want to use the feet for another project, wait for your creation to dry and then ask an adult to carefully cut the clay with a sharp knife so you can take it off.

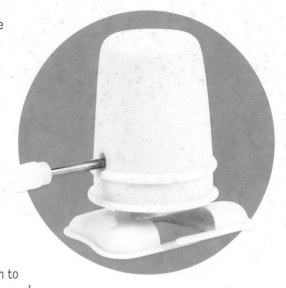

Once your clay creature is finished, just wind it up and let it go! Try racing a monster and an alien, or an alien and a robot to see which one is faster. Or race your creation against a friend's!

Annie Argh

Annie is a monster who likes tradition. She hides behind closet doors and scares small children, just like her parents and grandparents did.

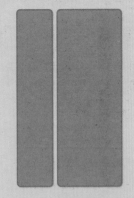

1. Wrap a 4 x 1.5-inch pink piece around the upper part of the walking base and smooth it out. Wrap a 4 x ½-inch strip around the bottom part.

2. Make 2 teardrop shapes for the arms and stick them on. Then make a big pink ball and squish it flat for the bottom part of the eye.

3. Roll out a white ball and a smaller black ball. Squish them both flat and layer them over the pink eye piece. Then give Annie a long, silly tongue!

4. Make 2 tiny white circles and stick them on the black of the eye for highlights. Make lots of little spots for this creepy (but lovable) monster!

Zappi

Zappi is kind of a trickster. If you fall victim to pranks like the glued-down coin or having your shoelaces tied together, you can bet this joker is to blame.

Pieces:

BODY

HEAD

EARS

EYES

TEETH

BELLY

1. Wrap a 4 x 1.5-inch blue piece around the walking base and smooth it out. Stick a round head on top and use one of your tools to press a smile into the clay.

2. Make 2 teardrop shapes for Zappi's arms and stick them on. Add 2 long flattened ovals for ears. Press a few tiny white circles into his mouth for a goofy grin.

3. Roll out 2 small yellow balls, squish them flat and stick them onto the head to make the bottom parts of the eyes. Make a flat dome shape for Zappi's yellow belly and stick it on.

4. Finish off the eyes by adding little white and black circles. Carve some lines into the stomach piece with one of your tools, then stick on some thin yellow pieces to make Zappi stripy all over!

Steve McBolt

Steve was designed to be a waiter in a Hollywood restaurant, but he dreams of becoming an action movie star.

Pieces:

BODY

HEAD

TEETH

EYES

ARMS

HANDS

CHEST

ANTENNAE

1. Wrap a 4 x 1.5-inch green piece around the walking base and smooth it out. Roll out 2 black tubes and wrap one around the top and one around the bottom. Stick a round head on top.

2. Add a black circle on each side of Steve's body, near the top. Stick 2 black circles on his head for eyes. Add a white strip for his teeth and a flat white square on his chest for a cool digital screen.

3. Roll out 2 long, thin cylinders for arms and attach them to the black circles. Stick a small black ball at the end of each. Then make Steve some antennae so he can receive signals!

4. For the hands, make 2 balls and cut into them with the straight-edge tool to make a little wedge in each. Stick them onto the arms. Add the white and black circles to the eyes, and a design on the screen.

17

Sayonara Sam

Sam escaped from a robotics lab by putting on a lab coat and pretending he was one of the scientists. His current whereabouts are unknown.

Pieces:

BODY

HEAD

EYES

ARMS

ANTENNA

HANDS

CHEST

TEETH

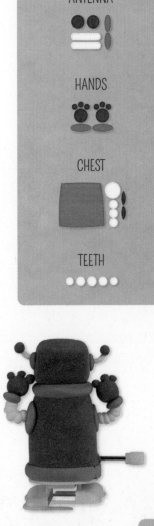

1. Wrap a 4 x 1.5-inch blue piece around the walking base and smooth it out. Roll out 2 orange tubes and wrap one around the top and one around the bottom. Stick a cube-shaped head on top.

2. Stick a small orange circle on each side of Sam's head, and a slightly larger orange circle on each side of his body near the top. Add 2 little white circles to the head and an orange square to the chest.

3. For each arm, make 5 little white balls and squish them together, then stick the arms onto the orange circles. Stick a pair of antennae on the head. Press in a few little white teeth for a wacky grin.

4. For each hand, stick 3 tiny blue balls onto a larger ball. Attach the hands to the arms. Stick tiny blue circles onto the eyeballs for pupils. Now add some buttons and an emblem to give Sam a cool look!

19

Bob the Blob

Bob the Blob floats around in the atmosphere of Saturn. He loves to gaze out at the rings that surround his home planet.

Pieces:

BODY

ARMS

HAIR

EYES

PUPILS

1. To make Bob's blobby body, roll out a ball then flatten it a little at the bottom. Press one of your tools into the clay to make the mouth.

2. Make flattened teardrop shapes for Bob's arms, then stick one on each side of his body. Make two flat triangle shapes for the tufts of hair and stick them on top of his head.

3. Make a bunch of tiny round balls in different sizes, squish them a bit and press them all over Bob's body to make spots. Next make 2 little white balls, flatten them and press them onto the front of the body for eyes.

4. Make two little black balls and press them onto the eyes for pupils. You can put one higher than the other to give Bob a silly look!

Lizzie

Lizzie the monster doesn't really like scaring people. She spends her days trying to see how many crackers she can stuff into her mouth at one time.

Pieces:

BODY

FEET

EARS

TAIL

EYES

TOOTH

1. Roll out a round ball for the body (Lizzie is basically a beach ball with feet!). Use one of your tools to press a smile into the clay. Roll out a long teardrop shape for a tail.

2. Make some flattened teardrop shapes for her pointy ears and stick them on her head. Make 4 little balls for feet and stick them on the bottom along with the tail.

3. Roll out 2 little balls of white clay, flatten them and stick them on for the eyes. Make a tiny little white ball and stick it in the mouth to give Lizzie a cute little snaggle tooth.

4. Finish off by rolling out 2 tiny black balls and flattening them. You can stick them on unevenly to give Lizzie a silly look. Finally roll out a bunch of tiny green balls in different sizes to make Liz super spotty!

Felix

Felix was an accidental stowaway on Apollo 11's return voyage from the moon. It took him a long time to adjust to his new life as an optometrist on Earth.

BODY

LEGS

EYES

PUPILS

TONGUE

TAIL

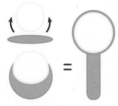

1. Make 2 small white balls. Next make 2 flattened green circles and wrap them around the eyeballs. Roll out 2 short cylinders and stick them on to make the eye stalks.

2. Roll a round ball to make Felix's body, and use one of your tools to create a mouth. Attach 2 teardrop shapes to the bottom for feet, and a smaller teardrop to the back for a waggly tail.

3. Stick the eye stalks to the body. It helps hold everything together if the eyes are touching at the top. Make a flat oval tongue and stick the end into Felix's mouth.

4. Stick 2 tiny black circles onto the eyeballs. Now make a bunch of tiny balls with dark green and stick them all over!

Wanda

Wanda is a big celebrity throughout the galaxy. She's lending her star power to the campaign for getting Pluto recognized as a planet again.

back leg side view:

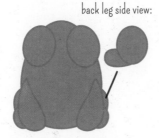

1. Roll out an egg shape for the body. Make two teardrop shapes for the front legs and stick them on.

2. For each of the back legs, roll out a ball and a teardrop shape and stick them together. Roll out a long teardrop shape for the tail and two flattened circles for bottom layer of the eyes. Stick all the pieces on.

3. Make some flattened circles with white clay that are a little bit smaller than the pink eye circles. Use one of your tools to press an indent into the clay for a big mouth, and press in about 6 tiny white pieces of clay for the teeth.

4. Make about 6 flattened teardrop shapes in different sizes for the spikes. Put the biggest one on top of the head and then stick them down Wanda's back and tail from largest to smallest. Rawr!

Monty

Monty used to be just a regular fish swimming around. But then a nuclear disaster made him into a mutant!

Pieces:

BODY

MOUTH

LEGS

TAIL

EYES

1. Roll out a ball of red clay. Roll out a small ball of pink clay and flatten it, then stick it onto Monty's front.

2. Make 4 teardrop shapes and stick 2 on either side, as shown in the side view photo below. Use a tool with a straight edge to make a couple of lines in each fin.

3. Roll out 3 little balls of white, flatten them and stick them on for the eyes. Make 3 small cylinder shapes and attach them at the back for the tail fin.

4. Make 3 tiny black balls, squish them and stick them onto the eyes. Make a small black oval and stick it on for a big, gaping mutant fish mouth!

Marcus

Marcus lives under your bed—augh! He's not so bad, though, just look at those big round eyes...er, eye.

BODY

FEET

1. Make a round ball for Marcus' body, then use one of your tools to give him a wide mouth. Make 2 little oval balls for feet, squish them a little and stick them on the bottom of the body.

2. Make 2 flat ovals for ears, and a couple of teardrop shapes for arms. Stick them onto Marcus' body.

ARMS

EARS

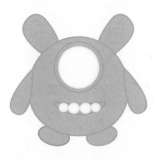

TEETH

3. Make 4 tiny round balls for the teeth and press them into the mouth. For the eye, you'll need a flat orange circle and a slightly smaller flat white circle.

4. Add a tiny black circle and a really bitty white circle to the eye. Then roll out some tiny yellow balls, flatten them and stick them on for Marcus' spots. Boo!

EYE

Dotty

Dotty is Marcus' cute little girlfriend. They totally have eyes for each other!

Pieces:

HEAD

BODY

FEET

ARMS

TAIL

EARS

EYE

BELLY

1. Make a big round oval for the head, and a round body that's a bit flattened at the top and bottom. Stick the head onto the body. Use one of your tools to give Dotty a smile.

2. Make two little balls for Dotty's feet and use a tool with a straight edge to create toes. Make 2 teardrop shapes for the arms and a flattened circle for the bottom part of the eye. Stick all the pieces on.

3. Roll out a small white ball and flatten it for the eyeball. Roll out a light pink oval and flatten it for the belly. Make 2 flattened ovals for the ears and a long teardrop for the tail. Stick all the pieces on.

4. Roll out a little black ball and a tiny white ball. Flatten them and stick them on top of the eye. Roll out a bunch of tiny light pink balls, flatten them and stick them all over to make spots.

Luella

When Luella was a little monster, she dreamed of becoming a prima ballerina. Sadly, her tail always got in the way, so she became a lion tamer instead.

Pieces:

BODY

NOSE

EARS

BELLY

LEGS

TAIL

EYES

TONGUE

1. Make a pink egg shape for the body and use one of your tools to press a mouth into the clay. Right above the mouth, stick on a small bit of clay for her little pug nose.

2. Make 2 narrow ovals for the ears and stick them on top of Luella's head. Roll out 2 teardrop shapes for her back legs and stick them on like in the photo.

3. Make 2 more teardrop shapes for the front legs and stick them on. Then give Luella a long waggly tail. With dark pink, make a flat half-moon shape for the belly and stick it on. Then add 2 flat white circles for her eyes.

4. Finish off the eyes by sticking on 2 tiny black circles. Now make Luella look funny by giving her a flat oval tongue sticking out of her mouth! Finish off by giving her a whole bunch of dark pink spots.

Space Rover

Rover is a loyal pet alien from Mars. She's happiest when she's playing fetch across the Martian surface.

BODY

LEGS

TAIL

BELLY

EARS

EYES

1. Roll out a round head and an egg-shaped body and stick them together. Use a tool to press a smile into the clay.

2. For the belly, roll out an oval and then flatten it and stick it onto Rover's front. Make the 5 teardrop shapes for the legs and tail, then look at the photos to place them.

3. Make two small white balls and squish them, then stick them onto Rover's head. For the ears, stick together 2 small light purple ovals and 2 slightly larger dark purple ovals. Attach the ears to the top of the head.

4. Add 2 tiny black circles to the eyes for pupils. Then use your tools to give her belly some stripes. Now you have your own cute pet alien!

Garett

When students in a university created Garett, they didn't expect him to become an artist. His paintings are now on display in the Museum of Modern Art.

1. Make a box shape for the head and an oval for the body and stick them together.

2. Roll out 2 teardrop shapes for the arms, and give him 2 rounded legs. If you want, you can give him a power pack on his back like in photo.

3. Make some little cone shapes for antennae and stick them on top of the head. You can put a piece of spiral wire between them if you want. Make 2 flattened circles to start the eyes.

4. Add little black circles and tiny grey circles to complete the eyes. Then be sure to give Garett a little heart on his chest! Finish off by using your pointy tool to poke some holes in the clay for seams.

Pieces:

Robbie

Robbie was given a heart so that he could feel emotions like a real person. He sometimes cries when he goes to the opera.

Pieces:

HEAD

NECK

BODY

HANDS & FEET

LEGS   ARMS

EYES

HEART

1. Make a larger cube for the body and a smaller cube for the head. Attach the head to the body with a small ball in a different color.

2. Poke a bunch of little holes around the edges to make it look like Robbie has screws holding him together.

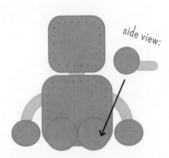

side view:

3. Make little balls for his feet and hands, and short cylinders for legs and arms. Attach the hands to the arms and the arms to the body. Attach the feet to the legs and the legs to the body.

4. Make 2 little white circles and press them onto Robbie's face, then stick black circles on top. Make a little heart to stick on his chest, and Robbie is ready!

Bort

Bort turned out to be much smarter than the people who made him. He went on to win a Nobel Prize in physics!

Pieces:

HEAD

BODY

LEGS

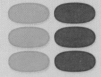

ARMS

HANDS

EYES

HEART

1. Make 3 box shapes in different sizes and colors. Stick the smaller 2 together for the body and stick the biggest one on top for the head.

2. Squish 3 balls together to make each of Bort's short little legs.

3. Squish 6 balls together for each arm. For the hands, make 2 slightly larger balls and cut into them with the straight-edge tool to make a little wedge in each. Stick the hands onto the arms.

4. Use the pointy tool to poke some holes for seams. Press 2 white circles onto Bort's head for eyes. You can make them different sizes to make him look silly! Add some black pupils to the eyes, and a little white heart on the chest.

Squiggy

Squiggy likes to vacation in hot places. You can usually find her sunbathing on the scorching sands of Mercury.

BASE

TENTACLES

HEAD

NECK BAND

EYES

1. Roll out a small cylinder and 6–8 long, thin teardrop shapes. Start attaching the teardrop shapes to the cylinder at their wide ends.

2. As you add more tentacles, bend and twirl the ends to make Squiggy look like she's moving.

3. Roll out a round ball and stick it on top for the head. Use one of your tools to press a mouth into the clay. Make a long pink tube to wrap around Squiggy's neck, between the head and tentacles.

4. Add some white and black circles for Squiggy's big eyes. Finally, make a bunch of little spots and stick them all over.

Making Plants

Once you've made a monster or alien or two, it can be fun to create a little scene for them like in the photos you'll see in the book. Try making some plants to give your creations a nice home to live in.

Cactus

1. Roll out 3 cylinder shapes in different sizes.

2. Stand them up on your work surface and press their sides together.

3. Use the pointy tool to poke a few holes all over.

Succulent

1. Make 8 little teardrop shapes. Flatten them and join them into a circle.

2. Bend the points upward. Make 6 slightly smaller shapes and add them on top of the first layer.

3. Make 4 more teardrop shapes, slightly smaller than before, and add them on top. Bend all the points upward.

4. Make a little ball and press it into the middle of the plant to close the gap.

Cactus with flowers

1. Roll out a ball and flatten it slightly. Set it on its edge and press down a bit so that it stands.

2. Make the other 2 segments the same way and stick them on top.

3. Roll out some tiny pink balls and stick them on for the flowers.

4. Use the pointy tool to poke a few holes all over.

Grass

1. Roll out about 10 or so long pointy shapes.

2. Start sticking them together at the wide ends.

3. Keep going until you're happy with your plant. Bend all the tips down slightly.

You can even make little clay leaves and stick them onto twigs to make tiny trees!